CW00520514

GOD'S NOT COOL

GOD'S NOT COOL

CHRISTOPHER MEGALLY

GOD'S NOT COOL

Copyright © 2018 by Christopher Megally.

Typesetting and Cover design by Sandy Yousef

ISBN-13: 978-1723180156 (CreateSpace-Assigned)

ISBN-10: 1723180157

First Edition: September 2018

This book goes out to anyone seeking to live the best life.

This life is not easy, but it is satisfying and gives hope for what's to come. I especially want to dedicate this to all my friends and family who might be struggling with their faith or maybe do not believe at all. I pray this causes a stir in your heart for change.

You are loved.

. . .

Contents

PREFACE

I think I can tell you exactly what you're thinking right now. "Chris, why is this book called god's not cool? Aren't you a Christian!?" I am. I am a Christian stating what most people in today's society think: God's not cool, I don't need him. It is an unfortunate point that we have reached in our society. Something like getting super drunk at parties and smoking weed has become so acceptable, and rather a big requirement in order to fit in.

What do I mean? Today, if you went around on the street asking people what they thought of God, you'd probably get responses telling you that they don't believe, don't care, or, no response at all. Especially with the younger generation, it almost seems as if God is someone shameful to talk about. But, why? I believe people have been presented with an image of God that is maybe misguided. It seems to be that the influence surrounding the upcoming generation is just too strong. This influence being that of partying, drugs, sex, money; all things harmful for any human being. In fact, to be "accepted" in today's world or be seen as "'cool", you fit that description when you get so drunk that it leads to an absurd Instagram or snapchat post that just shows you embarrassing yourself in front of everyone. Before all that, you need to take nice pictures, post them on Instagram with a nice caption showing everyone that you ARE busy and you HAVE a life.

With all this, we are all so blinded by the only thing that matters most: Jesus. Sound familiar? He's the God who laid his life down, so that we can be reconciled to Him. People can easily think of Jesus and go not cool, lame, boring, irrelevant, and turn to what's beside them, and move on. Let's tackle that together.

CHAPTER ONE

False Reality

Ah, these have probably become my two favourite words recently. False reality is what social media is today. False reality is also what society teaches you is fulfilling, ultimately leading to destruction. Instagram, Snapchat, Facebook, and YouTube are all telling you that having lots of money is happiness. They convince you that driving a fancy car and living in Hollywood Hills is happiness. So, something simple I like to do is analyze just a few people who "had it all" and unfortunately, plummeted to the ground. My first example is Robin Williams. He was a great actor and impacted many lives, and it's fair to say that he had everything. Fame, money, riches, you name it! Unfortunately, his life ended with suicide. Kurt Cobain is another notable individual who took his own life. Tony Scott, Jovan Belcher, Lucy Gordon, and the list goes on. Why am I talking about these people? They all had one thing in common: they had everything people are striving to achieve today. Countless young people today want money and fancy cars. This is where social media can become conflicting. Look at the enormous amounts of people who include their wealth in their online posts to show off. Look at how people react to these posts wishing they had expensive cars and nice clothing. Apparently, you are truly worth something if you're driving the latest Mercedes or if your house is greater than 2,500 square feet. I want you to think about all these famous people who "had it all" and despite all of it, took their own lives. One of the biggest problems people are not noticing today is that everything we are taught about true happiness is false. Every single detail of it; the entire concept this society pitches to you is wrong and deceiving. The same can be said about pornography. Now, relax and listen to what I have to say. Pornography is relevant in that when you look at porn, you are given a false image of what sex truly is in terms of the physical features and the fame. You are taught that the standard for a beautiful woman/ man is one that is curvy, has abs, long, shiny legs, and whatever other ideas you come up with in your head. The same exact problem arises when we turn on our phones and open the closest social media application. You see a picture of your friend on vacation and think "if only I could be there now". Your best friend posts a picture with his new car and you think "I'd love to have something like that". Instantly, your mind is hungry for more. You desire more items, more money, and nothing you have will ever be enough.

So, how can I prove to you that this is all false

reality of what true happiness is? Put it to the test. Picked up a new phone? It must feel great. You're probably so excited right now that all you want to do is use it and show people. Okay, and then, two weeks from now? How about a month? Your phone is just, well, a phone. Ah, but let's not forget, you got a new car! Wow, fantastic. You're driving it all day, taking your friends out, and embracing every moment. Two weeks go by, a month, two months, and you're sick of it. Admit it! This is what happens to us! We always want more, and every void inside of us will never be completely filled without Jesus. But we'll get to that in chapter two.

Why does this happen? Why does our feeling of fulfillment end so quickly? A lot of us tend to forget that one day we will die. Yes, we will die. As I write this, I laugh, because frankly none of us enjoy thinking about death. It is unfortunate, but true. Our time here on earth is so limited. Too many of us are living for the now, the latest, the greatest, the fancy, the expensive. Let's think about this. When you die, what goes with you? Everything you've ever lived to achieve is going to be gone. I don't want you to misinterpret what I'm saying. You CAN dream, you CAN achieve and frankly, you should. God, who made us, put dreams in us and desires that can be good and can be used to do good. The problem arises when we place our hope in the things of this world. I think it is fair to end this chapter with a line from the song "Alive" by Hillsong Young and Free, which goes; "Everything of this world will fade, I'm pressing on till I see your face". With that, I'll add 1 Timothy 6:6-7 which says "6 But godliness with contentment is great gain. 7 For we brought nothing into the world, and we can take nothing out of it."

CHAPTER TWO

Jesus Satisfies

It all goes back to how we were designed. Satisfaction is found in Jesus and only Jesus. I think it's fair to say that our whole lives are spent chasing certain goals. It ranges from athletic achievements, asking someone on a date, getting a new video game, getting a new bike; the list never ends. Let me move forward with you: you have now established that nothing in your life will ever satisfy you. Now think about Jesus: how can he satisfy you? Is it true that if I surrender my life to him, I might actually have true joy? The answer all sits in the word of God itself. Psalm 107:9 says "For he satisfies the longing soul, and the hungry soul he fills with good things". The simple idea that our souls are never satisfied by the things of this world tells us that we were made for something greater – ETERNITY.

Eternity with Jesus is the end of pain, suffering, hunger, thirst. It is the end of everything bad and the start of everything good. Alright, I'll answer your question now. How can Jesus satisfy me, Chris? Read the Bible. John 6:35, Jesus says "I am the bread of life; whoever comes to me shall not hunger, and whoever believes in me shall never thirst." You have to ask him, you have to seek him first and repeat verses like these back to him. People think that a connection with God is a one-way relationship. Jesus, however, returns with answers and promises through people and circumstances. I will repeat Psalm 107:9 "For he satisfies the longing soul, and the hungry soul he fills with good things." Isn't that beautiful? Now, don't take the hunger part literally. The hunger mentioned in the bible refers to our daily hunger for more. We are constantly seeking something to make us happy and to keep a big smile on our faces. We have an unending desire to find something or someone that will fix our problems. Psalm 22:26 "The afflicted shall eat and be satisfied; those who seek him shall praise the Lord! May your hearts live forever!" Make sure you focus on this one. Let me provide you with some context. The majority of Psalms were written by a man named David. When you dive into the book of Psalms, it has countless amounts of beautiful things being said about God. David constantly says how God is his defender, how he protects us, how he loves us, and how he is powerful. Psalms is extremely mind-blowing when you establish that the text written is from a human. Process that for a second; David is so in love with God that he wrote over 100 chapters about him, stating his promises and giving examples of how God protected him. Now is a good time to go "wow".

Finally, I present Psalm 16:11 "In your presence

there is fullness of joy; at your right hand are pleasures forevermore." This is what we want. As human beings, we want joy! Again, don't confuse the pleasures mentioned here as earthly pleasures. It is not to say God will not give you things in life – he could and does for many people. The main takeaway here is that with the word pleasures, the meaning refers to the pleasure of peace, joy, satisfaction, and everything that is truly good for us.

Let me tell you a story. One time I was working and during work, this girl noticed I was always over the moon. Big smile on my face, every shift, as if nothing could ever bring me down. So, one day, interestingly enough, she asks me "Chris, are you always this happy?" and with an even bigger smile I go, "all the time!". "How? Can you teach me how to be this happy? Like, I try every day, but it never seems to work". I answered with one word; "Jesus". From there on, me and this girl would continue to have conversations about Jesus, and it's crazy how he worked and allowed our friendship to grow and gave me opportunities to preach the gospel to her.

If you're reading this now and you aren't a follower of Christ, I want you to know something. This is too real to be an illusion. I was once presented with an argument that "Christians just convince themselves that God exists so that they can have faith in something and be happy". I stood there rather shocked. I know people can convince themselves of a lie, but that only lasts so long. The beauty of God is that he never fails you and if you just ask him, he will respond. The way God sees it is that he has an unending hunger for you to turn to him. So, when you ask, why won't he respond? He might not respond instantly, but he will at the perfect time, and when he does, you will know it.

One of the greatest quotes I ever read was written by C.S. Lewis. "The fact that my soul is never satisfied and always longs for something more, tells me that I was made for something greater" In short, nothing of this world was ever meant to satisfy us anyways. As humans, all we truly want but forget, is eternal peace and joy. We long for a pain and worry-free life. Notice how all I've said is still perfectly in tune with what I mentioned in chapter 1. Had anything in this world been adequately satisfying for the soul, would all those big names like Robin Williams still have taken their own lives? Use those individuals as examples to show you that only one person can and will satisfy you, if you ask: Jesus.

CHAPTER THREE

Social Media

I 'd like to say that the biggest problem the world faces today is how impactful social media has become. The problem is that so much is being thrown at teenagers and young adults, that all we can do is consume. With this, we find ourselves being so distracted because one minute its YouTube and the next its scrolling through our Instagram feed. In recent times,

I noticed how fixated people are on showing others what is happening in their life.

This is so sad, and so consuming, that it simply breaks my heart.

As a matter of fact, due to all the destruction I felt was happening in my own life, I deleted it all. Yup, you read that right. I deleted snapchat, twitter, all of it. My phone is for the simple use of pictures and videos, along with messaging, done! Can I tell you something? And don't keep it a secret? Its changed my life so much in an amazing way. I'll admit, when I first took the step to delete everything, I was worried I'd miss out on a lot. I thought I'd miss out on people's lives and anything funny that goes by. Now, vice versa, I also think about how much life I was missing out on; time with family, enjoying good weather, friends, even working out. I noticed that so many of us glue our faces to our phones and scroll through snapchat stories without thinking of all the time we are wasting. It's a bigger deal than you think, and its scarier than you realize.

So, what happened then? What happened when I

deleted it all? Freedom. A breath of fresh air. No more need to reply to inboxes on Instagram, no hours wasted on my phone. Just me, God, and the enjoyment of family and life in general. The more I was away from social media, the more critical I became on others and the time they spent on it. What's even better, was that not for one second was I envious of them. Not for a minute did I think "I want to download it all again". I was free and I LOVED it.

Why do I think Social media is a huge problem? Why do I think it's at least 85% of the problem? Because it's on social media where we are fed false reality. It's on social media where we come across so many different opinions, views, problems, that we struggle to develop and form our own view. It's on social media that we aspire to be LIKE others. Since we are all so surrounded by these things, time flies and we find ourselves day in and out missing on the one thing that will satisfy us completely. The Bible is filled with incredible documents of stories that happened, verses of encouragement, and examples that we can relate to in our life today. It feeds you, it has what you're craving, but that you don't know you're craving.

As I think back, I'm tempted to change my percentages. Instead of social media being 85% of the problem, I want to split it 50/50. The other 50% is the image people have of God. Digest that for a second. In today's world, if you went over and asked hundreds, thousands, millions of people about God that don't know God, the answers would all roughly sound the same. They would probably have claimed to be raised in a Christian household, and then lost interest, grew out of church, got into partying and drugs, and now their god is money, sex, fame, etc.

CHAPTER FOUR

Relation, Not Religion

This is a common misconception people have on Christianity. This is also a very big reason people consider God "lame" or "not cool". Before I give my two cents on denominations, let me give a disclaimer: I do not hate anyone. I am simply bold about what I believe and feel I have good reason to believe so. Most people today have been part of or come across many different churches who share different beliefs regarding God. There are countless denominations such as Coptic, Catholic, Presbyterian, the list goes on. The problem with this is that we can become so focused on denominations and how to please God with our different rituals, that we forget about relation.

Denominations. What are they and why do they exist? How do they harm the church? They harm the church because they don't act like one. With denominations, you get people that are convinced that "they're right and everyone else is wrong". So, you have conflict. You have an uproar of disagreements and different ideas. For decades, you have different denominations interpreting what is said in the bible differently and creating their own ideas of it.

As I think of it, it strikes me as to how big of a problem denominations are in Christianity. I will say that in my view of things, denominations are what caused people to look at God and say "hah, lame"; or look at him with zero interest.

The blame does not fully go to the different

denominations, but it is a big portion of it. As these different sectors of Christianity grow, they develop new rules and rituals, leading people to consider Christianity "just another religion". It not only breaks my heart but fumes the fire in me to preach the gospel to as many people as I can, however I can.

You see, once I established that God simply wants to love me and once I confessed what I've done wrong, it not only blew me away but took me to my knees. You don't need to live up to any standard with Jesus. You don't need to make sacrifices and repeat a scripted prayer five times. All he wants is for you to LOVE him! Isn't that amazing? He has commandments he wants you to follow that all lead to one thing: LOVE. His word speaks so much truth that it shows his love for you! There are verses that instill confidence in you and verses that remind you God is FOR you and that he is your SHIELD! I mean, can I just get an amen? God's word is not only so true, but so uplifting and satisfying.

Before I get carried away more, let me step back to denominations again. So many churches today are so concerned with following the rules they've made and the routines they've established that they simply forget to stress solely on the word of God. It is extremely difficult today to find a church with an unapologetic pastor who whole heartedly preaches what the Bible has to say with absolutely no regret or holding back. It is what we lack, and we need it! Instead, what do we find? A repetition of stand up, sit down, close your eyes, repeat after the priest.

I'll give you my unapologetic ending: most churches don't do enough. I personally believe that the reason so many people have a negative idea of God and who he is because of their experiences at church. I am in no way saying that the church experience needs to be made in a way to cater to others, but the church simply needs to be truthful. It needs to be Bible focused and Bible focused only. It needs to be loving and respectful; it cannot be filled with man-made rituals. The church must be the word of God alone, and if that is done, everything changes. You will have an army of Christ that is not only powerful, but filled with so much love and confidence that they want to share with the world. You will have the younger upcoming generation, who are dealing with so many obstacles, look to Jesus to overcome their problems. You will truly and simply find yourself building the Kingdom of Heaven here on earth. I want to also add that part of what drifts people away from God is the sacrifice. As human beings, our flesh enjoys the negative areas in our lives. For some odd reason, to which I hope to find out one day, we actually do enjoy being depressed, angry, bitter, and simply in a state of darkness. We don't want to leave our comfort zone, which is exactly what a relationship with God is all about. When you enter your relationship with God, you give him the wheel. You sit in the passenger's seat, buckle up, and trust him as the driver. With that, you give him all your struggles and seek for him to help you. Unfortunately, when you are so caught up in the flesh, you don't want to do that. You find yourself simply not able to trust God and move on. This is where you have to take that risk, take a step. You need to stop hating yourself and the position you're in and start seeking real help. You need Gods help and his help only. You have nothing to lose, so ask him. That's our issue as a society; we do not ask, we do not seek, and so we will not find. We do not want the good side, we oddly do not want peace and freedom from our torment. Take that step now, realize that your constant cycle of pain, dissatisfaction, fighting, anger, sadness and hurt is not taking you anywhere. Jesus is calling, and he's waiting for you to pick up and walk with him. Matthew 7:7 "Ask and it will be given to you, seek and you will find, knock and the door will be opened".

CHAPTER FIVE

Eternity

Eternity is one concept people forget to think about. It is something people forget is real. Have you ever played a game in which you got any sort of item that was "permanent"? There was most likely some level of excitement with that right? That feeling that a specific item is yours forever and will not go anywhere unless you or the game dies, literally. Think of eternity: it is forever. Eternity does not end, it does not fade, and nothing can kill it. Eternity is what comes after this life. So easily, as human beings, we forget this truth. I want you to sit and think about it for a second. If eternity is real, if there is life after this one on earth, what is it like? Where do we go?

I'll tell you about two places that exist outside of this world, heaven and hell. Heaven is where Jesus is, and it's where all his followers will go after life here on earth. Heaven is the thing that encourages us Christians to not fear death but try to face it with confidence because of our assurance of where we will go after. Hell is simply the opposite. Hell is the eternal separation from the God of love. With this, I am not here to try and tell you about the gospel because hell is bad, I am here to tell you the gospel because of how good God is. If you're reading this book, you are reading it because God wants you to. He has a message for you that is being sent through me. Life here on earth might seem pretty and nice, and thankfully it is for a lot of us. But it ends. Just like all things on earth, it ends. I'm so sorry to say it, but frankly I can't control it. Now think, because it ends, what should I do next? I want you to truly think of what you live for. This society always paints a picture of what looks good: the sex, the money, the fame, the luxury. They feed you with lies that all die when you die too. Imagine this - you are the next big thing. You have the nicest cars, you're 500 followers short of 2 million on twitter, you have it all! You live in a nice house in Los Angeles and your girlfriend/boyfriend is smoking hot. Alright, awesome.

Now what? You want more, don't you? It's not enough. Then, you get the newest iPhone and more expensive clothing, but, it's just not enough. You keep going only to realize that not only does this stuff not satisfy, but it is all worthless. When you die, your Gucci bag isn't taking a trip with you to heaven. When you die, your 2 million twitter followers don't hang around either. None of it counts for anything, especially for God. When you see God face to face, and you present to him your Bentley and your 10-million-dollar mansion, he will disregard it faster than the speed of light. It all ends, and that is the main thing you need to take from this. It ends! Read these next lines very carefully. This life ends, and there is one that comes after it.

The reality is, after this life, it does not just go "black". It isn't that we all go to one place. It is not that we are separated as "good people go here and bad go there" but both have it good still. There is a life after this. Well, there could be, you just need to believe. What is so amazing about God is he has no requirements for you other than to believe. He isn't asking for rituals, scripted prayers, special actions. All Jesus wants is for you to believe. John 3:16 "for whoever believes in me shall not perish but have eternal life". It is simply incredible to ask so, so little of someone.

When I think of eternity, I find it so hard to accept that people tend to hold onto time way so desperately. It's all about pretending like life isn't real sometimes. A lot of us pretend like one day we don't die. As I am writing this, just yesterday, I went to church and part of the sermon was on salvation. It is truly crazy how many people live in the spotlight today and think it lasts forever. Countless individuals think that they are some sort of god and everything that matters is here on earth. People forget that you can't keep your heart beating forever. Science won't be able to do it. Death is inevitable. I want to take you through a little test right now.

I want you to ask yourself what exactly you're living for. I want you to think of how much the world has offered you that has pleased you. Be honest with me and yourself. Has anything of this world truly satisfied you regardless of your circumstances? Has this person/thing completely filled you with joy regardless of your circumstances? Has this thing really gotten you through the tough times, or are you just convincing yourself it has?

I want you to give God a chance. Not in a testing way, but humbly and respectfully. Yep, right now,. Even if you don't believe a God exists, I want you to humble yourself and ask him something. "Lord, I am at a point in my life where nothing seems to satisfy. I've tried it all, I have relied on my own will. Nothing has satisfied me, and I am filled with mixed emotions that never fade.

Please reveal yourself to me and help me". Now before I go any further, I don't want you to think there is going to be an instant response. For some, there could be. Just be patient. Seek him and you will find. Knock and the door will be opened. Trust me when I say that, Jesus speaks to us in very interesting ways. When he speaks to you, you'll know it and feel it. Ask for specific things, be eager, ask God all your questions. He loves them, and it is your right to be curious but respectfully. Don't test God, but rather seek him with a humble attitude.

I would like to end with another unapologetic statement. One day, you and I will die. Gosh, sometimes I hate to think about it but it is a reality, isn't it? Where do you want to be? If I told you right now that heaven and hell really do exist, what would you choose? Would you not want to be eternally satisfied with peace and joy? Would you not want to live your life here on earth differently? Eternity is important, and with that, I'm sure you've been seeking a better life here on earth. God offers that. He doesn't promise to make it easy, but he offers joy. He IS joy! He is your shield that will protect you through the struggles and the light that will shine in the darkness. I strongly, strongly encourage you to consider all I am saying. Forget the religious systems and trying to meet certain standards. Christianity is more. Forget religion and think relation. All of humanity is desperate for all these things but some simply do not know it. If you're reading this now, it's because God loves you and wants to speak to you. Don't let it go by.

CHAPTER SIX

The Step

At this point I'd say the question that comes begging is "why Jesus?" and "why do I need him?". Romans 3:23 states "for all have sinned and fallen short of the glory of God". This is extremely powerful and true because of what today's society is so fixated on. Every day its focused-on being "good people" and doing "good things". The truth that no one likes to hear is that no matter how good you might think you are, you're still a sinner. So, what makes us sinners? How are we always sinful? Ever since the very beginning with Adam and Eve, sin was formed and instantly we were separated from God, hence our need for him. Now you might think "well, Chris, how is this fair if I must pay for the sins of two people?". With that, I will present two crucial points. The first being that God gave us all a way out of our sin in the first place. God being God could have easily left us for dead and not even considered dying for us to save us from our sins, yet he did. The second, which ties in very closely to the first, is that God also gives us an outstanding reward for turning away from sin, and he makes it easy. The process is simple; believe in Jesus and you shall not perish but have eternal life.

Life isn't a game, and it shouldn't be treated as one. We all pass. Whether we like it or not, we will all pass. We NEED God's love and mercy to save us. Why? We are always sinful. Whether it is through our thoughts or actions, sin is always present even without us knowing it. I always like to consider this life we live as a second chance. Actually, let me correct myself: our zillionth chance. Every single day, waking up and being able to live is another chance at life. We are not in control and never will be. This statement is not something new to you, but I will never understand why so many people are holding onto time with a firm grip. We pretend like this never ends; we simply act ignorant to the fact that our new iPhone will not count for anything.

Our Gucci clothing and tesla will go when we do. We must take THE STEP of courage and the step of humbling ourselves before God and admitting we need him. Forget all material things, and look at how many people today are looking for hope. Endless numbers of people are so hopeless that they kill themselves, while so many others are discontent and constantly angry. Countless people are indulging in their sin thinking it will satisfy but always end up disappointed. The step' towards a new life in Christ is not easy but it is a free gift. Just try this now with me. humble yourself Close your eyes and ask God; "God, whether I believe you exist or do not, putting my doubts and judgements aside, I ask for your help. Please, reveal yourself to me in any way that you please. You know my heart, you know me better than I know myself. Show me true freedom, show me why I need you. I ask this in your name. Amen".

See how simple that was? This is not to say the Christian walk is easy, but is it not mind blowing how God gives us this free gift? Would it not be nice to be sure of your life after this one instead of living in doubt? I encourage you to not be misled by this society into thinking that this life is what matters most. You need to understand something – I am all for fun, I enjoy life as much as I can. I am all for do rather than don't. What I am saying though, is be smart. What this society wants is for you to conform to every rule that they come up with.You are convinced that having expensive clothing and cars is what will make you happy. You think that being high class means being a king or queen. That is NOT true. Wake up and realize what world we actually live in. Stop claiming life is short but living as if it will be around forever. God loves you so much that he is

trying to give you a wakeup call, and if you don't need it, then maybe a loved one you know does!

We've come to the end of this journey together. I want to end this book with something from my heart. I truly wrote this book with every intention for readers to become saved and move from their old self to a new self in Christ. I am 100% sure God will use this book to speak to people, even if it is just one. I want you to know that, I, along with billions of other people out there have had amazing life changes. All the details I've heard before in testimonies remind me that there is an artist at work who is specifically drawing out each person's life. Gods message of love and forgiveness is what really changed me from an angry and lustful person, to a teddy bear who hates sin. I couldn't make this change on my own, I cannot convince myself of all this. It is real change that happened. I want YOU, the reader, to have this change!

I can't give it to you, and I can't start it, only God can. I said it before, and let me say it again; Ask and it will be given, seek and you will find, knock and the door will be opened!

ACKNOWLEDGEMENTS

God – Thank you for changing my life and speaking through me while writing this book. I am so grateful for all that has changed in my life, and I love you dearly for all you do for me.

Danial, thanks for half editing my book and then forgetting it even existed! You rock bro

Sandy, thanks for editing my whole book and helping me set up everything! You are awesome

Dimo, my brother, thank you for editing my book as well with such deep thought and honesty. Your tips were extremely helpful, and my book got better because of you

Androu, thank you for the conversation we had before finalizing my book which gave me more insight into what a relationship with God truly encompasses. God has given you a gift my brother, always use it

Finally, thank YOU the reader for reading my book. You obviously read this because you had some sort of interest in doing so. I hope it was worth your time, and I hope you got something out of it. God bless you always, my friend!

Made in the USA
Columbia, SC
30 September 2018